U.S. PRESIDENTS MYTHS OR FACTS?

MYTHS AND FACTS ABOUT ULYSSES S. GRANT

EZRA E. KNOPP

PowerKiDS press

Published in 2024 by The Rosen Publishing Group, Inc.
2544 Clinton Street, Buffalo, NY 14224

First Edition

Editor: Greg Roza
Book Design: Michael Flynn

Photo Credits: Cover Werkat/Shutterstock.com; (series background) Azamatovic/Shutterstock.com; p. 5 ItzaVU/Shutterstock.com; p. 7 https://commons.wikimedia.org/wiki/File:Ulysses_Grant_at_21.jpg; p. 9 https://commons.wikimedia.org/wiki/File:Robert_E_Lee_1838.jpg; p. 11 Zack Frank/Shutterstock.com; pp. 13, 15 (Mary Todd Lincoln), 15 (Julia Grant) Everett Collection/Shutterstock.com; p. 17 https://en.wikipedia.org/?title=File:Ulysses_S._Grant_Trapeze_Cartoon_Keppler_Puck_1880.tif&page=1; p. 19 courtesy of the Library of Congress; p. 20 Wangkun Jia/Shutterstock.com.

Library of Congress Cataloging-in-Publication Data

Names: Knopp, Ezra E., author.
Title: Myths and facts about Ulysses S. Grant / Ezra E. Knopp.
Description: Buffalo : PowerKids Press, [2024] | Series: U.S. presidents : myths or facts? | Includes bibliographical references and index.
Identifiers: LCCN 2023032249 (print) | LCCN 2023032250 (ebook) | ISBN 9781499444087 (library binding) | ISBN 9781499444070 (paperback) | ISBN 9781499444070 (ebook)
Subjects: LCSH: Grant, Ulysses S. (Ulysses Simpson), 1822-1885–Juvenile literature. | Presidents–United States–Biography–Juvenile literature. | United States–History–Civil War, 1861-1865–Juvenile literature.
Classification: LCC E672 .K73 2024 (print) | LCC E672 (ebook) | DDC 973.8/2092 [B]–dc23/eng/20230712
LC record available at https://lccn.loc.gov/2023032249
LC ebook record available at https://lccn.loc.gov/2023032250

Manufactured in the United States of America

CPSIA Compliance Information: Batch #CWPK24. For Further Information contact Rosen Publishing at 1-800-237-9932.

CONTENTS

WHAT'S HIS NAME?

Ulysses S. Grant was born April 27, 1822, in Point Pleasant, Ohio. Grant's father, Jesse Grant, was a hard-working **tanner**. Ulysses Grant learned some of the dangerous, or unsafe, trade at an early age, but he didn't like it.

Instead, Grant worked on farmland his father owned. At a very young age, he became well known in the area for handling difficult horses. Reports say that by the time Grant was 10 years old, he was regularly driving a carriage and team of horses 45 miles (72.4 km) away and back.

IT'S A FACT!

HAVE YOU EVER HEARD THE CLASSIC JOKE: "WHO'S BURIED IN GRANT'S TOMB?" YOU CAN FIND THE PUNCHLINE AT THE END OF THIS BOOK!

A STATUE OF GRANT ON HORSEBACK STANDS WATCH OVER THE U.S. CAPITOL BUILDING IN WASHINGTON, D.C.

MYTH OR FACT?

"ULYSSES" WASN'T ULYSSES S. GRANT'S FIRST NAME.

FACT

Grant's actual name was Hiram Ulysses Grant. So why did people call him Ulysses S. Grant?

Grant decided that he'd rather go to college than work on a farm. In 1839, with the aid of a friend, Grant's father got him into the U.S. Military Academy at West Point. However, the friend reported that Grant's name was Ulysses Simpson Grant. (Simpson was his mother's family name.) Although Grant tried to change the name at first, he realized the initials "U.S.G." would look better on his uniform than "H.U.G."!

IT'S A FACT!

BECAUSE OF HIS NEW INITIALS, GRANT BECAME KNOWN AS "UNCLE SAM" GRANT. HIS CLASSMATES CALLED HIM "SAM."

GRANT DIDN'T LIKE THE WEST POINT UNIFORM. OBSERVERS NOTED THAT HE OFTEN WORE THE UNIFORM IMPROPERLY. IN FACT, GRANT DISLIKED WEARING FORMAL CLOTHING FOR MOST OF HIS LIFE.

MYTH OR FACT?

GRANT, FUTURE LEADER OF THE UNION ARMIES DURING THE AMERICAN CIVIL WAR, ATTENDED THE SAME SCHOOL THAT THE FUTURE LEADER OF THE CONFEDERATE ARMIES ATTENDED.

FACT

Grant didn't want to join the military. However, he quickly realized it might be his only chance to continue his education and to travel. Grant was an average student. He did very well in math and **equestrian** training. He filled his spare time with art classes and classic books. In 1843, Grant graduated 21st out of a class of 39.

Someone Grant would one day meet in battle also attended West Point. That man, Robert E. Lee, would later become the leader of the Confederate army during the Civil War.

IT'S A FACT!

GRANT AND LEE DIDN'T MEET AT WEST POINT. THEY WOULD, HOWEVER, MEET AT THE END OF THE CIVIL WAR—WHEN GENERAL LEE **SURRENDERED** TO GENERAL GRANT!

WHILE LEE WAS AT WEST POINT (1825–1829), THE OTHER CADETS, OR STUDENTS, CALLED HIM THE "MARBLE MODEL" BECAUSE HE WAS SUCH A GOOD STUDENT.

BUSINESS AND WAR MYTH OR FACT?

GRANT WAS A VERY SUCCESSFUL BUSINESSMAN.

MYTH

Grant was successful as a soldier and officer during the Mexican-American War. However, he was not happy in the military, and he **resigned** in 1854. He wanted to become a businessman.

Grant, his wife (Julia Dent), and their two sons moved to the Dent family farm near St. Louis, Missouri. Julia's father gave Grant 80 acres (32 ha) of land to farm. The farm failed. In 1860, Grant worked in his family's leather goods store in Galena, Illinois. Grant's bad luck in business would follow him throughout his life.

IT'S A FACT!

SOME THINK GRANT'S FARM COULD HAVE BEEN SUCCESSFUL HAD HE USED ENSLAVED LABOR. JULIA'S FATHER GAVE HIM AN ENSLAVED MAN TO WORK THE FARM, BUT GRANT GRANTED THE MAN HIS FREEDOM.

TODAY, THE ULYSSES S. GRANT NATIONAL HISTORIC SITE STANDS ON PART OF THE FARM WHERE GRANT WORKED.

MYTH OR FACT?

GRANT MADE SURE ROBERT E. LEE WAS CHARGED WITH TREASON AFTER THE END OF THE AMERICAN CIVIL WAR.

MYTH

During the American Civil War, Grant again found success as a leader. He was given a particularly unruly group of soldiers and reformed them. After Grant won numerous victories in battle and several promotions, President Abraham Lincoln made him lieutenant general of the Union armies in 1864.

On April 9, 1865, when Lee and other Confederate leaders surrendered to Grant at Appomattox Courthouse in Virginia, Grant showed **leniency**. He let them keep their horses and return to their homes. Grant felt this was important to lasting peace.

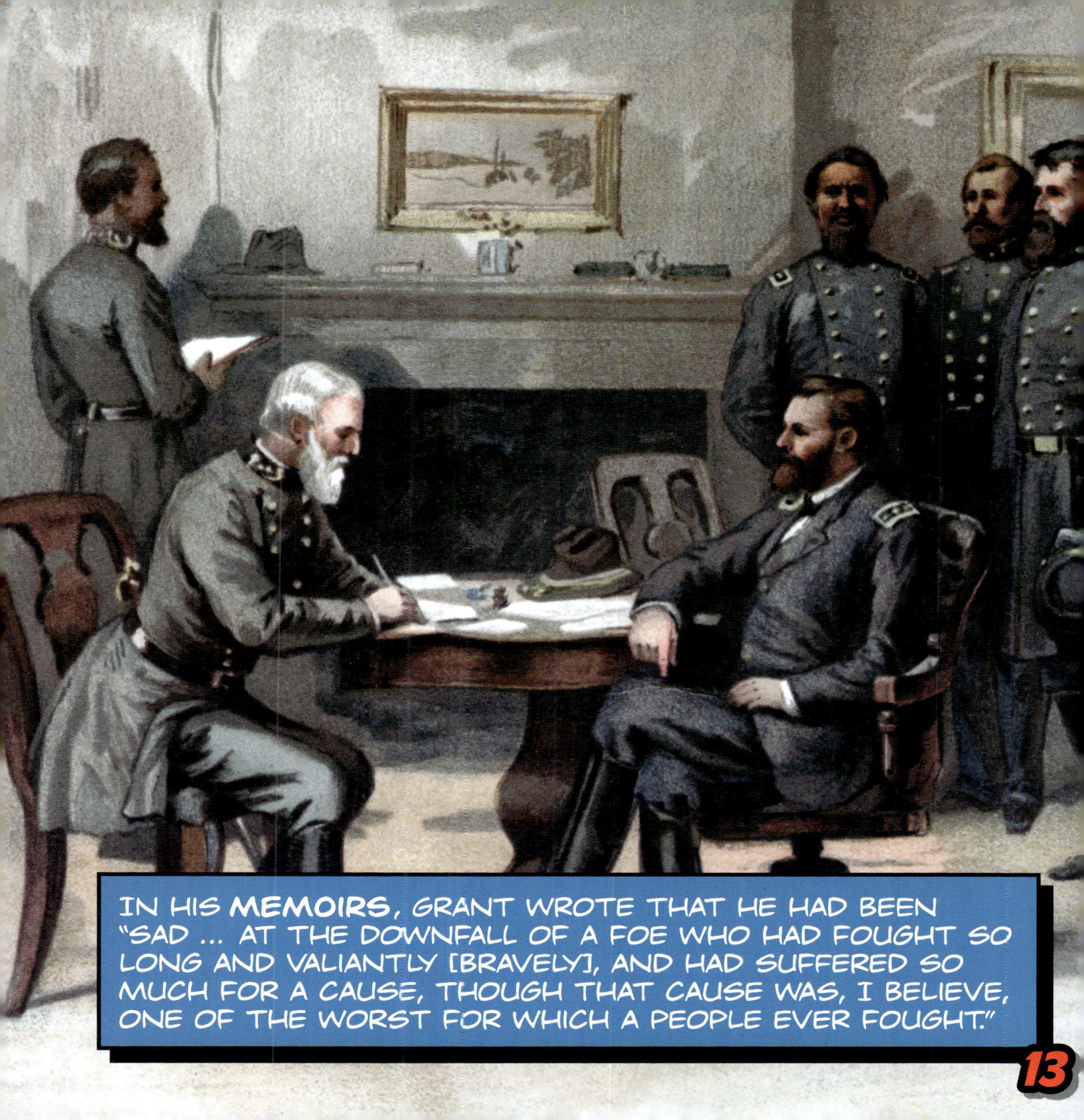

IN HIS **MEMOIRS**, GRANT WROTE THAT HE HAD BEEN "SAD ... AT THE DOWNFALL OF A FOE WHO HAD FOUGHT SO LONG AND VALIANTLY [BRAVELY], AND HAD SUFFERED SO MUCH FOR A CAUSE, THOUGH THAT CAUSE WAS, I BELIEVE, ONE OF THE WORST FOR WHICH A PEOPLE EVER FOUGHT."

MYTH OR FACT?

PRESIDENT ABRAHAM LINCOLN HAD INVITED GRANT TO THE THEATER ON THE DAY HE WAS ASSASSINATED, BUT THEIR WIVES DIDN'T GET ALONG.

FACT

On April 14, 1865, President Lincoln had invited Grant and his wife, Julia, to join him and his wife, Mary, at Ford's Theatre in Washington, D.C. Grant declined the offer, stating that he and his wife planned to visit their children.

Historic reports are clear that Julia Grant didn't like Mary Todd Lincoln. Mary's anger and competitiveness were **notorious** around Washington, D.C.! Reports show that Mary had insulted Julia at a previous gathering. As a result, Julia asked her husband not to attend the play.

IT'S A FACT!

LINCOLN AND GRANT CAME TO RESPECT EACH OTHER DURING THE CIVIL WAR. THEY HAD SIMILAR CHILDHOODS AND THOUGHTS ABOUT THE COUNTRY. GRANT WROTE THAT LINCOLN'S DEATH WAS THE "DARKEST DAY OF MY LIFE."

MARY TODD LINCOLN

JULIA GRANT

A JOURNALIST ONCE REPORTED THAT MARY TODD LINCOLN YELLED AT JULIA GRANT FOR SITTING WHILE SHE WAS STANDING! MARY SHOUTED, "HOW DARE YOU BE SEATED UNTIL I INVITE YOU!"

PRESIDENT GRANT MYTH OR FACT?

GRANT WAS LARGELY INEFFECTIVE AS A PRESIDENT.

MYTH

When Grant became president in 1869, he took over a still-divided country from Andrew Johnson. Johnson hadn't cared to fix the problems between the North and the South. Grant, however, wanted to preserve the Union and promote **Reconstruction**.

During his two terms, Grant fought to protect freed enslaved people and worked to pass the 15th **Amendment** to the U.S. Constitution. He used federal troops to fight hate groups in the South. He also spoke out for more **humane** treatment of Native Americans.

IT'S A FACT!

IN HIS BIOGRAPHY OF ULYSSES S. GRANT, *GRANT* (2016), AMERICAN HISTORIAN RON CHERNOW STATES THAT, "GRANT DESERVES AN HONORED PLACE IN AMERICAN HISTORY, SECOND ONLY TO LINCOLN, FOR WHAT HE DID FOR THE FREED SLAVES."

MUCH OF GRANT'S TWO TERMS AS PRESIDENT WERE MARKED WITH **CORRUPTION**, AS THIS POLITICAL CARTOON SUGGESTS. MANY OF GRANT'S FELLOW POLITICIANS, INCLUDING HIS OWN BROTHER, ORVIL, WERE ACCUSED OF TAKING MONEY AND GIFTS IN RETURN FOR POLITICAL FAVORS.

MYTH OR FACT?

GRANT WAS ARRESTED FOR SPEEDING IN A HORSE-DRAWN CARRIAGE THROUGH WASHINGTON, D.C., WHEN HE WAS PRESIDENT.

FACT

A newspaper report from 1871 shows that Washington, D.C., police were on the watch for racing carriage drivers due to recent accidents. One day, Grant himself was pulled over for speeding! He apologized to the officer and promised not to do it again.

However, the very next day, the same officer pulled Grant over for leading a carriage race! Grant was taken to the police department, where he paid a fine of $20. The report says Grant was amused to see his fellow racers, also politicians, complain about their arrests.

THE $20 GRANT PAID WAS TO MAKE SURE HE APPEARED IN COURT. HE DIDN'T APPEAR IN COURT AND SO LOST THE MONEY, BUT HE DID PRAISE THE POLICEMAN FOR HIS COURAGE TO MAKE ARRESTS AND KEEP PEOPLE SAFE.

GRANT'S TOMB

After his presidency, Grant began writing his memoirs. Writer Mark Twain offered to publish the book. Grant finished his memoirs just a few days before dying of cancer on July 23, 1885. The book sold very well.

The General Grant National Memorial is the final resting place for Grant and his wife. It's a mausoleum, or an aboveground grave. Comedian Groucho Marx used to ask, "Who's buried in Grant's Tomb?" Since the Grants weren't buried, the answer is "No one." However, Groucho would also accept the answer "The Grants."

GRANT'S TIMELINE

APRIL 27, 1822	HIRAM ULYSSES GRANT IS BORN IN POINT PLEASANT, OHIO.
1843	GRANT GRADUATES FROM WEST POINT.
1848	GRANT AND JULIA DENT MARRY.
1854	GRANT RESIGNS FROM THE MILITARY AND BEGINS FARMING ON HIS FATHER-IN-LAW'S ESTATE.
1861	THE AMERICAN CIVIL WAR BEGINS. GRANT JOINS THE UNION ARMY IN APRIL AND RISES THROUGH THE RANKS TO BECOME LIEUTENANT GENERAL OF THE UNION ARMIES.
APRIL 9, 1865	ROBERT E. LEE SURRENDERS TO GRANT AT APPOMATTOX COURTHOUSE IN VIRGINIA, ENDING THE CIVIL WAR.
MARCH 4, 1869	GRANT BECOMES THE 18TH PRESIDENT OF THE UNITED STATES.
FEBRUARY 3, 1870	GRANT SIGNS THE 15TH AMENDMENT TO THE CONSTITUTION, GIVING BLACK MEN THE RIGHT TO VOTE.
NOVEMBER 5, 1872	GRANT IS REELECTED PRESIDENT.
JULY 23, 1885	GRANT DIES.

GLOSSARY

amendment: A change in the words or meaning of a law or document, such as a constitution.

corruption: Illegal or dishonest behavior by government officials.

equestrian: Having to do with horses.

humane: Kind and good to others.

leniency: A lack of severe (great) punishment for doing something wrong.

memoir: A story of personal experiences; an autobiography.

notorious: Widely and unfavorably known.

Reconstruction: The period from 1865 to 1877 in which the Southern states that had seceded during the American Civil War rejoined the United States.

resign: To quit.

surrender: To give up.

tanner: A trade-person who tans, or uses chemicals, to prepare animal hides for leather production.

treason: The crime of attempting to overthrow the government of one's country.

FOR MORE INFORMATION

BOOKS

Gains, Ann. *Ulysses S. Grant: Our 18th President*. Parker, CO: Childs World, 2020.

Lowe, Lindsey. *Ulysses S. Grant and Robert E. Lee: Rivals of the Civil War.* Buffalo, NY: Enslow Publishing, 2023.

Rumsch, Breann. *Ulysses S. Grant*. Minnesota, MN: Checkerboard Press, 2020.

WEBSITES

Biography: Ulysses S. Grant
www.ducksters.com/biography/uspresidents/ulyssessgrant.php
Learn a lot more about Grant on this detailed web page.

Ulysses S. Grant and Julia Dent Grant Exhibit
www.nps.gov/subjects/ulyssesgrantexhibit/index.htm
You can read much more about Grant, the places where he lived, and the people he knew at the National Park Service website.

Publisher's note to educators and parents: Our editors have carefully reviewed these websites to ensure that they are suitable for students. Many websites change frequently, however, and we cannot guarantee that a site's future contents will continue to meet our high standards of quality and educational value. Be advised that students should be closely supervised whenever they access the internet.

INDEX